FEATS of 21st-CENTURY ENGINEERING

21st-CENTURY AIRPLANES

Enslow Publishing
101 W. 23rd Street
Suite 240
New York, NY 10011
USA
enslow.com

Lisa Idzikowski

Published in 2019 by Enslow Publishing, LLC.
101 W. 23rd Street, Suite 240, New York, NY 10011

Library of Congress Cataloging-in-Publication Data

Names: Idzikowski, Lisa, author.
Title: 21st century airplanes / Lisa Idzikowski.
Other titles: Twenty-first century airplanes
Description: New York, NY : Enslow Publishing, 2019. | Series: Feats of 21st-century engineering | Includes bibliographical references and index. | Audience: 3-6.
Identifiers: LCCN 2017046147| ISBN 9780766096912 (library bound) | ISBN 9780766096929 (pbk.)
Subjects: LCSH: Airplanes—21st century—Juvenile literature. | Airplanes—History—Juvenile literature.
Classification: LCC TL547.I49 2019 | DDC 629.1333/34—dc23
LC record available at https://lccn.loc.gov/2017046147

Printed in the United States of America

To Our Readers: We have done our best to make sure all website addresses in this book were active and appropriate when we went to press. However, the author and the publisher have no control over and assume no liability for the material available on those websites or on any websites they may link to. Any comments or suggestions can be sent by email to customerservice@enslow.com.

Photo Credits: Cover, p. 1 (technical drawing) pluie_r/Shutterstock.com; cover, p. 1 (Nighthawk stealth fighter) Erik Simonsen/Photographer's Choice/Getty Images; p. 4 p_saranya/Shutterstock.com; pp. 9, 11 Bettmann/Getty Images; pp. 12–13 Universal History Archive/Universal Images Group/Getty Images; p. 17 Getty Images; pp. 18–19 NASA/Lockheed Martin/Cover Images/Newscom; pp. 21, 33 © AP Images; p. 23 Marc Garanger/Corbis Historical/Getty Images; pp. 26–27 VCG/Visual China Group/Getty Images; p. 29 Tom Tschida/NASA/SIPA/Newscom; pp. 30–31 Power Sport Images/Getty Images; pp. 36–37 Airbus/Cover Images/Newscom; pp. 38–39 NASA/MIT/Aurora Flight Sciences; p. 40 US Air Force Photo/Alamy Stock Photo.

CONTENTS

Thousands of people experience the thrill of flight every day. The planes of the future will make soaring above the clouds even more amazing!

Introduction

Flying machines have an interesting history. Throughout time, people imagined being able to fly. They observed birds in flight. They also studied windmills. Early on, the Chinese flew kites. Later, Italian artist and inventor Leonardo da Vinci drew detailed designs of flying machines. Years passed as experimentation blossomed in many areas of science and mathematics. Scientists and engineers identified and understood basic theories of motion. They calculated the mathematical formulas that would help make the science of flight possible in the future.

At the time of the Industrial Revolution (about 1760–1840) many new scientific and technological inventions appeared. Like engineers today, people of the time began to ask questions, define problems, and design and test possible solutions. Many of the pioneers of aviation were simply interested in flight. They were handy with tools and possessed a spirit of invention. Most designed, built, and tested their own model flying machines. Often these early models did not live up to expectations. What did these clever individuals do then? Instead of quitting, many worked harder. They found ways to improve their crafts through additional testing, data collection, and redesign.

During the mid- to late 1800s, several individuals dedicated their work to searching for ways to fly. They designed and built different types of aircraft. Some crafts flew, while others never even made it off the ground. Unfortunately, some aviators died when their experimental crafts crashed. Early flying machines and some pilots may have perished, but the engineering and data of those first flights became the rich ground for future experimentation. And in 1903, after nearly one hundred years of early attempts, Orville and Wilbur Wright made the first successful airplane flight.

From there, the science of flight, known as aeronautics, took off! An entire industry built upon early aeronautical successes jetted ahead. Flight schools sprang up. Universities began to establish engineering programs dedicated to aeronautics. The development of airplanes advanced during times of both war and peace.

Eventually, airplanes became a part of everyday life. They were used regularly to carry cargo and passengers alike. Aeronautical engineers designed new and improved aircraft. They incorporated aerodynamics, propulsion, materials, structures, and stability and control into the design process.

These innovations have not stopped. Improvements to airplanes and the field of aeronautics are always being sought. It is amazing and inspiring to glimpse into the future of aviation. The promise of aircraft that will be fast, fuel efficient, environmentally friendly, and safe is a splendid possibility!

1

How Did Humans Learn to Fly?

Orville and Wilbur Wright owe a debt of gratitude to the pioneering aviators that came before them. The Wright brothers looked at all that the early aviation inventors had accomplished. They worked hard to improve upon their ideas. They experimented with different designs until they got it right. Serious attempts at flight had started long before the two bicycle-shop owners turned their attention to flying and ended up changing history.

Pioneers in Aviation

By the early 1800s, Sir George Cayley was experimenting with flying machines. As a professional engineer, he knew the value of building models from theory, asking questions, testing with repeated trials, and collecting data. Cayley also communicated his findings by publishing articles in scientific journals. That way others could learn and benefit from his work. Cayley found that a cambered, or curved, wing was necessary to produce lift in an airplane. He built gliders that successfully carried the weight of a person in flight.

According to Wilbur Wright, one of the most important pioneers of flight was Otto Lilienthal. As a college-educated mechanical engineer,

Lilienthal understood the necessity of research, design, testing, data collection, and publication of results. He studied birds and their patterns of flight. His observations assured him that cambered wings would produce the best lift for man-made flying machines. He also convinced other researchers to apply mathematical rules to flight data. This proved helpful with further experimentation.

Lilienthal constructed sixteen varieties of gliders and completed almost two thousand flights, soaring through the skies of Germany. However, his gliders lacked mechanical control. To guide his craft, Lilienthal had to move his weight back and forth as he flew. When Orville and Wilbur Wright learned of Lilienthal's death in an accidental crash, they vowed to move ahead in their own efforts to produce a flying machine.

About this same time, Octave Chanute, a trained civil engineer, entered the field of aviation. Chanute believed that his experience building railroads, locomotives, and bridges would benefit the growing community of pioneer flyers. His glider designs looked a lot like the frame of a bridge. He flew his gliders in Indiana along the shores of Lake Michigan. Chanute concentrated on getting the word out about earlier designs and experiments with various flying machines. He gathered all the latest information into a book. He also presented lectures about what was happening in aviation. Orville and Wilbur Wright and many other pioneers of flight benefitted greatly from Chanute's efforts.

Samuel P. Langley was in the audience during one of Chanute's presentations, and he decided to join the ever-growing group of pioneering aviators. Langley was an astronomer. By the time he headed up the Smithsonian Institution in Washington, DC, he had built the first ever engine-powered, unpiloted model aircraft. The wood, metal, and silk craft, called Aerodrome No. 5, flew surprisingly well. But when Langley enlarged the model to full scale, the flying

Aviation pioneer Otto Lilienthal guides his glider on an experimental flight in 1891.

trials did not go well. His life-sized great Aerodrome failed miserably and fell into the water. As a result, Langley gave up his efforts and stopped his research and experimentation into flight.

Twelve Seconds Leads to History

Langley's setback did not dampen the enthusiasm of Orville and Wilbur Wright, however. From a young age both brothers were encouraged to follow their interests. Their mother made toys for her sons, as well as simple household machinery. From her, the boys learned how to build and fix things. Wilbur had a surprisingly good memory. He read all the books he could get his hands on. Orville appeared to be the budding inventor because he was forever taking things apart to see how they worked. Neither of the brothers was schooled in engineering. Like today's engineers, however, they looked at problems, asked questions, and tested multiple designs and solutions. Most important, if they failed they went back over their plans, checked for mistakes, and made improvements.

By 1896, as owners of the Wright Cycle Co. bicycle shop, Orville and Wilbur had several advantages over earlier aviation pioneers. They designed, built, and repaired bicycles. They stocked a large variety of materials, including all sorts of tools. The brothers not only had a knack for using tools, but they also devised new and different ways to use them. Their large shop had more than enough room to assemble their gliders. Building bicycles by hand had taught them to think about balance and control, construction with lightweight

Forces of Flight

The Wright brothers engineered the first flying machine because they successfully used the four aerodynamic forces of flight. Lift, weight, thrust, and drag are the forces—or the push and pull—that act on flying objects. Whether they are working in nature, like birds, or in man-made creations, such as aircraft, these four forces must be working together for flight to occur. Lift is the force that pushes the wings upward. Weight works against lift. It is the force of gravity pulling objects toward Earth. Flying objects move through air, and drag is the force resisting forward movement. Created by the aircraft's engines, the force of thrust counteracts drag and pushes a plane forward.

No. 821,393.

PATENTED MAY 22, 1906.

O. & W. WRIGHT.

FLYING MACHINE.

APPLICATION FILED MAR. 23, 1903.

3 SHEETS—SHEET 1.

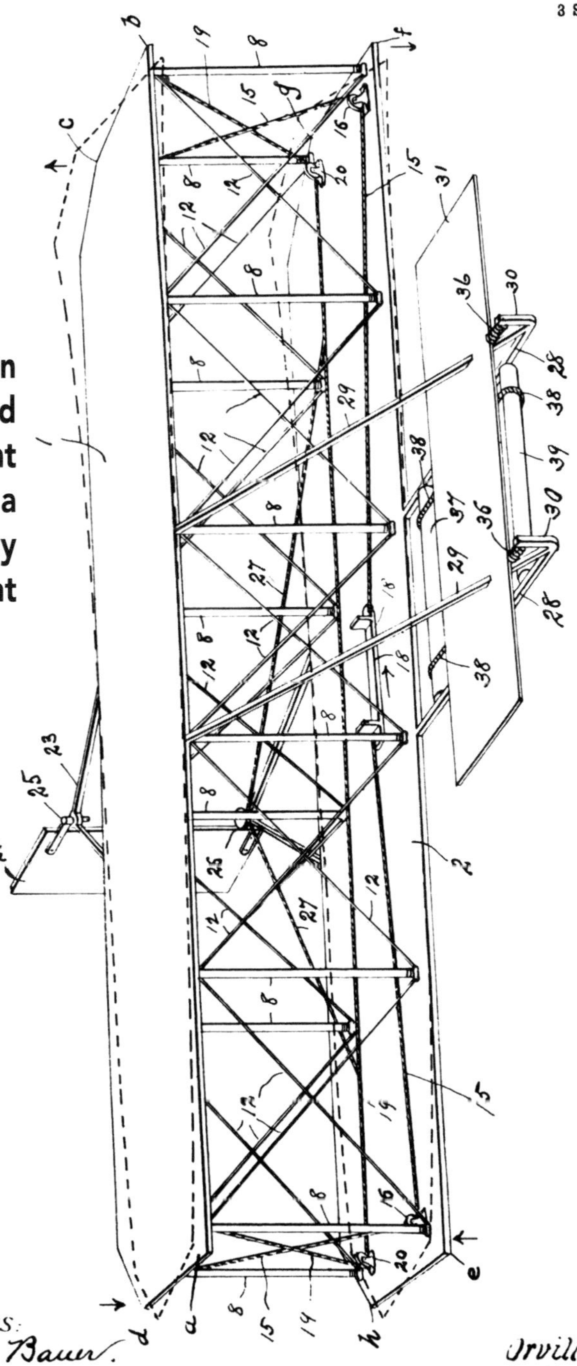

FIG. 1.

After a successful season with their most advanced glider in 1902, the Wright brothers applied for a patent. In 1906, they finally received a patent for their flying machine.

WITNESSES:
William F. Bauer.
Irvine Miller.

INVENTORS.
Orville Wright
Wilbur Wright
BY
H. A. Toulmin.
ATTORNEY.

materials, and using a system of chains and gears for moving forward. They would later use all of this knowledge to build their aircraft.

The brothers began their program in aviation with research. They read all the available books, articles, and materials that gave useful advice about earlier flying machines and experimentation. In 1899, Wilbur even wrote to the Smithsonian Institution telling them of his interest in flight. From this research, the brothers decided that flying

On December 17, 1903, in Kitty Hawk, North Carolina, the Wright brothers piloted the first controlled, powered flying machine.

came down to three important areas: the wings, a system of balancing and controlling the aircraft, and a way to propel the machine.

They began with balance and control. They reasoned that, just like a bike, a flying machine could be unstable but still controllable. They identified the problem, began testing ideas, and came up with a solution. Wing warping was the answer! This was a way to twist or angle the wings to maintain balance and also turn the craft. Borrowing from designs of the past, the brothers constructed a kite, fitted it with their original wing-warping system, and tested it. It was a success. They were happy that Wilbur could easily control the kite's movements.

Wilbur and Orville forged ahead. They built full-size gliders with space for a pilot. They found a new site for testing their craft. For the next two years, the Wright brothers flew, tested, modified, and retested their gliders at Kitty Hawk, North Carolina. For two flying seasons, Wilbur and Orville had nothing but troubling results. Problems occurred with lift and control. The frustrated pioneers kept questioning, checking calculations, making changes, and retesting the gliders.

Back home in Ohio, the brothers knew they had to try something different. They built a wind tunnel and created tools to test the forces of air on small model airplane wings. Test after test showed what they had guessed. Data and mathematical calculations from earlier experimenters had been flawed. The brothers kept at it. They designed, tested, and changed wing shapes. They added and connected parts for better overall control of the craft. By the fall of 1902 their efforts paid off—the Wright brothers launched their craft and took turns gliding, soaring, and turning the glider.

The Wright brothers had done it! Now it was time to add an engine and propeller and build an airplane. Orville and his bicycle company's mechanic had to design and make the engine and propeller from the bottom up. Before the next flying season, Orville and Wilbur finished their new powered flying machine, the *Flyer*. It was much larger and stronger than the gliders. They were excited to get to Kitty Hawk to test it. After fixing some minor details and waiting for better weather, Orville and Wilbur took their creation to the launching site. On December 17, 1903, Orville climbed aboard the *Flyer* and took the controls. At 10:35 AM, Orville and Flyer lifted off and sailed away, flying for twelve whole seconds.

The Wright brothers had worked with one goal in mind—a controlled, powered, flying machine. With the *Flyer* they had just flown into history!

2

The Need for Speed

Fast food, phones, internet, computers. Today, people want everything fast. That includes plane travel. Whether it's for business or pleasure, airline passengers are traveling more than ever, and they expect to get to their destinations quickly!

How Fast Is Fast?

Cruising along at about 768 miles per hour (1,236 kilometers per hour) is fast, but anything above that is *really* quick. Sound travels at about 768 mph. Planes flying above this speed, known as Mach 1, are traveling in the supersonic range. For several years, scientists and engineers at the National Aeronautics and Space Administration (NASA) and other companies have been testing several technologies to bring faster travel to our lives. The results of this research have been used on projects aimed at bringing back supersonic flight technology for commercial airline use. Research scientists and engineers from all the agencies are moving ahead with the challenges and are working through defined problems of supersonic flight so that we all can experience it one day!

The Four Speeds of Flight

There are four different speeds, or regimes, of flight. The regimes of flight are: subsonic, transonic, supersonic, and hypersonic. Most airliners that carry either passengers or cargo fly at the subsonic level. This is flight less than the speed of sound, or Mach 1. Aircraft flying at about Mach 1 are said to be transonic. Supersonic aircraft are flying at speeds greater than the speed of sound, or above Mach 1. Aircraft flying in the supersonic regime can fly at speeds from above Mach 1 up to Mach 5. A craft flying at speeds greater than Mach 5 is in the hypersonic range.

Too Fast to Believe!

Can you imagine flying across the United States from New York City to Los Angeles in less than one hour? That would be almost 4,000 miles per hour (6,400 kph). An important part of NASA's research is the program of aeronautics dedicated to hypersonic flight. For over twenty years, NASA researchers have been conducting experiments into super-fast flight using different experimental aircraft. They believe this experimentation will benefit general aviation in the United States. It also will help them design aircraft that will fly faster for transportation and for use in space. Researchers apply three systems to inform their investigations: wind tunnels, flight of X-planes, and computer software.

One project used the Pegasus Space Launch Vehicle to reach flight speeds of Mach 8 and collect data on airflow, heat, and drag. In the Hyper-X Program, scientists tested and gathered data of flights at Mach 7 and Mach 10. The last of the Hyper-X scramjet-powered planes reached a speed of Mach 9.6, or almost 7,000 miles per hour (11265 kph). Research continues with these incredibly fast craft.

NASA's X-43A hypersonic aircraft streaks through the air to break a world speed record.

A Supersonic Transport

Teams of engineers and scientists experiment with all areas of their Commercial Supersonic Technology (CST) projects. Their goal for the future is to bring back airliners that can travel across the United States, from New York to Los Angeles in about two hours. (This flight currently takes more than five hours.) In the beginning, scientists identified problems associated with supersonic aircraft. Researchers then decided to push their problem-solving efforts in the direction of noise reduction. Good thinking, since commercial supersonic craft that emit sonic booms are not allowed over US skies.

NASA

The Quiet Supersonic Transport, or QueSST, is being designed and tested to fly within supersonic range without creating sonic booms.

Besides testing, NASA has been busy working with designers to build an actual test model plane, or X-plane. After getting approval from the aeronautics and space agency, a private company developed an early model for the QueSST. This is a low boom experimental plane. Recently, the design passed wind tunnel trials. NASA hopes to begin flight testing of this plane by 2021.

BOOM's XB-1

Engineers at BOOM, a private aerospace company, have also taken up the challenge to produce a supersonic passenger aircraft. Why would anyone want to spend eight hours in flight when that time could be reduced to three to four hours, this company asks. Unlike NASA, BOOM concentrates its efforts on pure speed and time-saving flight. Its aim is to produce planes that regularly fly at Mach 2.2, or 1,451 miles per hour (2,300 kph). This is over two and a half times faster than ordinary airliners. To do this, research at BOOM has centered around flight science, improved engines, and lighter-weight materials for the structure of the plane.

BOOM's engineers have improved key features of previous supersonic planes to reach their goal. This includes making changes to the shape of the body, or fuselage, and also the wings. Researchers have also found solutions to the problems created by heat. Previous planes have been made from aluminum. BOOM engineers have come up with special materials, composites, that do not react to the increased temperatures of high-speed flight. To reach its projected Mach 2.2 speed, XB-1 will be propelled by three turbojet engines. These will be supplied with 7,000 pounds (3,175 kilograms) of jet fuel. The company is hoping that XB-1, or Baby Boom, will be in test flights by 2018.

AS2 is another supersonic passenger jet in the works. According to its creators, this aircraft could make the flight from New York to

Plans for the AS2 supersonic jet include commercial flights from New York to London.

London in a little more than four hours. This would save about three hours of traveling time over present jet flights. The AS2 is built to be fast. Engineers have made two important changes in general plane design to make this happen. The wings of AS2 are short and thin, and the body is long. Both the wings and body are made from special carbon material to be light and strong. By using this combination, the drag force is reduced so the aircraft can fly much faster than regularly designed jets. AS2 is expected to begin test flights by 2021.

Today's Fastest Aircraft

One of the fastest planes flying today is Air Force One. The aircraft that transports the president of the United States is also known as the flying oval office, or Angel. Air Force One can speed along at about 600 mph (965 kmh), which is close to the speed of sound. The current plane, a 747-200s made by US aeronautical company Boeing in 1990, will soon be replaced by a new and improved model, the 747-8s.

Supersonic Flight in the Past

From 1976 until 2003, a supersonic transport, or SST, carried passengers across the Atlantic Ocean in less than four hours. The British and French designed and built the Concorde, which took up to about one hundred passengers and flew at almost 1,400 miles an hour (2,253 kph).

Today's aeronautical engineers are attempting to design planes that don't have the problems of the Concorde, especially the high fuel use and loud noise. By developing better engines, fuel storage, and plane construction materials, researchers say that they have conquered the problems that the Concorde faced.

Long before the Concorde, US Air Force captain Charles E. "Chuck" Yeager piloted the first plane ever to fly faster than the

The supersonic Concorde completed its first test flight in the spring of 1969. Its last flight was on October 24, 2003.

speed of sound. Information uncovered from Nazi Germany and its flight experiments in World War II (1939–1945) prompted the United States to begin research into flight that was faster than sound. The US government contracted several companies to build test planes. Exciting newly designed aircraft tested various ideas of flight science. Aeronautical engineers of the time collected data, posed questions, and shared test results.

Bell Aircraft Corporation of New York built the XS-1 Experimental Sonic 1 plane in 1945. Bell's engineers designed the body of the plane after a bullet because bullets were known to travel at supersonic speeds after being fired. A rocket engine pushed the plane through the sound barrier.

On October 14, 1947, Chuck Yeager climbed aboard his XS-1, nicknamed Glamorous Glennis. Yeager and the test plane were carried into the sky by a B-29. After dropping out from under the carrier plane, Yeager ignited the rocket engines and zoomed through the sound barrier at Mach 1.06. Interestingly, this faster-than-sound flight was such a mystery that the XS-1 flight was labeled top secret. The public did not know about this record-breaking flight until reports leaked out to newspapers several months later.

3

Greener and Cleaner

Before we know it, tomorrow will be today. Airlines are expanding their fleets of planes to handle an ever-increasing number of passengers taking to the skies. To meet global standards that look out for the environment, planes must get "greener" and "cleaner." To get there, aeronautical engineers must define the problem and ask the right questions. They must apply research, design, problem solving, and testing to help produce aircraft that reach these clean targets of operation. Environmentally cleaner planes will be a winning plan for both passengers and for our planet!

Use Biofuels to Make It Clean

Governments, industries, and airlines in countries all over the world have been funding research programs to investigate biofuels for several years. Because biofuels are made from sources other than fossil fuels such as oil and coal, they are more sustainable and cleaner. Biofuels can be made from plants such as algae, or even from chicken fat!

Researchers began by asking this question: Can changing the makeup of jet fuel decrease damaging emissions? Research teams at NASA began testing their theory. They set up experiments to check

multiple types of biofuel. Scientists expected sustainable fuels to lower plane emissions. Now they had to prove their hunch was right.

An early trial involved a renewable fuel made from chicken fat. Researchers tested the biofuel on a DC-8 engine that was grounded, but running. They compared it to regular jet fuel and to a 50-50 mix of jet fuel and biofuel. The scientists' hunch proved correct. After collecting the data and working through the results, they found that chicken fat biofuel did burn cleaner in an airplane engine.

In a later experiment, scientists working together from Canada, Germany, and NASA set out to prove the same held true in the air. NASA's DC-8 aircraft flew as high as 40,000 feet (12,192 meters) powered by a mixture of regular jet fuel and a biofuel made from plant oil. Three other planes, including one from Canada and one from Germany, trailed the jet. Scientists collected emission samples and tested the results. After studying the data, researchers concluded that the plant oil biofuel also was a success.

The experiments proved that biofuels can reduce harmful greenhouse gas emissions by 50 to 70 percent! More testing is needed, but aeronautical researchers hope that jet planes will be powered by these mixtures in the future. Such airplanes will produce less pollution.

Private companies are also taking advantage of promising biofuel research. LanzaTech is one company in the United States that is

Biofuels (such as the sample in the container held by this worker) are being developed in the United States and around the world. In the future, planes will be powered by this cleaner type of fuel.

Flying on Algae?

Some planes are already flying on fuel mixtures that contain biofuel. As a renewable energy source, biofuels are made from living things and don't add greenhouse gasses to the air. One plant source being used to produce biofuel is algae. Like other plants, algae take in carbon dioxide from the air and give off oxygen during photosynthesis. But unlike other plants, algae produce a form of oil in their cells. It is this oil that is being tested for use as biofuel.

attempting to turn industrial waste products into usable biofuel. Through a special process developed by its scientists, gas is captured from steel mills and turned into fuel. LanzaTech's product is still in the testing process, but the company is working toward the day when its new fuel will be powering passenger planes.

To Go Green, Go Electric

Electricity is another source of airplane power that could help the environment. Aeronautical engineers hope that the same technology that pumps less pollution into the air from electric cars can be used for planes. Not long ago, NASA researchers began working on electric plane designs. Would it be possible to engineer electrically powered planes so that greenhouse gas emissions could be reduced or even eliminated, they wondered.

NASA scientists designed a research project using X-plane technology to test their theories. The X-57 aircraft, or Maxwell, was the first planned X-plane project in a decade. In four stages of experimentation, a Tecnam P2006T aircraft manufactured in Italy will undergo changes to its engines and wings. At each new stage, a research team will test several design variables. They hope to answer

Engineers and researchers at NASA work on an experimental craft. Powering planes with electric propulsion would produce cleaner, quieter aircraft.

the question of whether electric power will work. By the last stage of testing, the Maxwell will sport a new thin wing with fourteen electric motors—twelve high-lift motors and two large cruise motors.

Because the idea of electric planes is so new and different, NASA's scientists have formed special tools to work the bugs out of this new technology. With that in mind, pilots are also getting specialized training before flying these experimental planes. NASA has dedicated ten years to this electric program and hopes to have clean, electric-powered planes flying soon.

How Clean Are Today's Planes?

When planes burn less fuel the amount of emissions into the air decreases. Over many years, airline companies have been trying to design and build planes that are more energy efficient, which means their planes burn less fuel, give off less carbon gas, and cause less air pollution. Companies have also tried to reduce the amount of fuel their planes use because airplane fuel is expensive. Overall, planes now fly about one-half mile on a gallon of fuel. This is an increase in fuel efficiency of about 40 percent since 2000.

One of the largest airline companies in the United States, the Boeing Company, has been designing and building planes for over one hundred years. Its engineers are always searching for ways to improve their aircraft. They have made huge advances in fuel use. Comparing the jets Boeing built in 1960 to the 787 Dreamliners of today, the newest jets are about 20 percent more fuel efficient. To achieve this goal, aeronautical researchers at the company have gone through years of experimentation. The newest technologies have improved their aircraft.

Europe's Airbus also aims to make its planes friendlier towards the environment. With continual research, testing, and improved designs, its newest planes, the A 350s, fly with a greater fuel efficiency. According to Airbus, this group of planes is the most technologically advanced. One exceptional feature is their curved winglet. This added feature makes it possible for a plane to use less fuel in flight. Improvements to the wings, engines, and special construction materials make the A 350 lighter in weight overall. With all of these

An Airbus A350 XWB aircraft soars through the skies. The curve of the wing helps cut down on fuel.

engineered improvements, Airbus 350s can fly with an average 25 percent lower fuel use. This is excellent for the environment!

Are Quiet Planes Possible?

Aeronautical engineers have been searching for a solution to deliver quieter planes. Noise pollution is a problem, especially in neighborhoods near airports. Everyone wants the benefits of airplanes, but without the noise. The aviation industry is working to design quieter engines and landing gear.

One experimental craft has shown that quieter planes are possible. This is the BWB, or blended wind body plane. Researchers and designers from Boeing and NASA have worked together on this project. This X-plane, the X-48C, looks like a sea creature. It is flat, shaped like a manta ray, and has no tail, and the engines are placed at the rear of the craft. The research team is happy so far with test data that show this design creates less noise.

Bringing back supersonic flight is a dream for many in the aviation community. But there continues to be one big problem with these aircraft: sonic booms created by shock waves. Researchers are devoting time and effort to solve the problem. Until the noise problem is solved, these supersonic planes will not be allowed to fly over land in some countries.

Early testing used F-18 jet aircraft flying overhead at an air base in California. Volunteers on the ground rated their feelings on sonic booms that reached them from the planes. Another type of testing involved special photography to create images of the shock waves from sonic booms. This is often done in wind tunnels, but using high-speed camera equipment in natural environments is possible. Researchers found that using desert vegetation as a backdrop can produce good photographs. Scientists have also developed software that maps the location and intensity of sonic booms. In the future, this

It's a bird! It's a plane! It's Boeing's X-48 Blended Wing Body research aircraft.

technology may be used to direct the booms to less populated areas and decrease upsets to affected communities.

Recently another round of testing has begun over the skies of Florida. Engineers hope to use data obtained from this new program, called SonicBAT, to improve their designs and decrease sonic booms. Engineers have used data from SonicBAT testing done over dry desert areas. Now they want to see what happens in the warm humid air over the Florida coast. Research teams will continue working to reduce the problems of noise pollution.

4

The Future of Airplanes

Aviation has come a long way since the days of Otto Lilienthal's glider. Scientists and engineers continue their research to make aircraft faster, quieter, and cleaner for the environment. New technologies are being developed every day. Technology has already given us self-driving cars and smartphones. What's next for the future of flight—smart planes, self-driving planes, and space planes?

Self-Flying Aircraft?

If the idea of self-driving cars makes you nervous, hold on to your hat! The future is set to have self-driving planes. Many aviation companies have used a system of basic autopilot for decades. But now with advanced technology and software, some airlines are testing computer systems that will go above and beyond the basic autopilot.

Several private aeronautical companies are getting into this act. Boeing is betting on artificial intelligence, or AI, to totally replace some human pilots. The company estimates that in the next twenty years or so, about 1.5 million pilots will be needed to cover the expected increase in flights. It hopes that AI will cover the expected shortage. Ground testing of the new technology has already begun, and Boeing hopes to be flight testing within a couple years.

Meet the megacity transport vehicle of the future. The Pop.Up maneuvers through traffic on the ground but can take to the air to avoid congested areas.

Aviation giant Airbus has teamed up with Italian engineering company Italdesign to produce an autonomous, or self-driving, self-flying vehicle called the Pop.Up. It sees this machine as a car that can beat the traffic jams of large cities by popping up propellers, detaching from the wheels, and flying off.

NASA is also in the game of testing unmanned aircraft systems and the use of artificial intelligence. It is working with the Federal Aviation Administration (FAA) to set up ways that unmanned craft can fly in the same skies as ordinary planes. Interested people from around the world came to see recent test flights of NASA's new aircraft. Research teams at the space agency are also experimenting with AI. They hope to produce a system that will help pilots make decisions in emergency situations. This could reduce the number of human errors. After testing is complete and bugs are worked out, this technology may help pilots turn a bad situation into a happy ending.

Here Comes a Cool Future!

Can you imagine controlling a flying machine just by thinking? It sounds like science fiction, but researchers at the University of Minnesota have found a way to do just that. This technology is based on a specially designed device worn as a cap. Using electrodes, the device picks up signals sent from the brain of the person wearing the cap. As the person wearing the cap thinks about a certain movement, a signal is sent to the computer. Through Wi-Fi, the computer then directs the flying machine. Almost magically, the machine flies!

Within a few decades, commercial airplanes could take on a whole new look!

One type of futuristic design in development is the Double Bubble, D8 series. This craft comes from a research team at the Massachusetts Institute of Technology. Researchers at MIT were concerned with finding a way to reduce the force of drag, which acts to slow a plane down in flight. To find a solution they developed the Double Bubble, which has an extra-wide body made of special

lightweight material. Three engines are located on the tail in the back. NASA has been helping with the study of this craft and is testing it and others like it in its wind tunnel. In a best-case scenario, it hopes to be flying these models as X-planes in the next decade.

Some scientists have their sights set on the stars, or at least planes that travel to space and back. Kevin Bowcutt, a researcher at Boeing, sees a new propulsion system that includes scramjets as the way ahead. He has been heading up design teams behind hypersonic flight experiments. A few years ago, one of his designs, the X-51A WaveRider, set the record—three and one-half minutes at Mach 5.1—for a hypersonic craft. Right now, it is terribly expensive to fly into space. But with the right design, an aircraft that could be used again and again would lower costs. This could make plane flight into space affordable for many people.

Dan Newman, another scientist at Boeing, sees a future filled with rotorcraft, similar to helicopters. Newman imagines rotorcrafts parked in driveways of the future. Imagine a four-hour car ride to Grandma's house for Sunday dinner turning into a forty-minute flight!

A similar craft is being constructed by the firm Lilium, in Germany. This company wants its clean, quiet, electric jet to become an affordable air taxi of the future. This craft takes off vertically but then levels out to horizontal flight. The craft would allow as many as five people to travel five times faster than in a car! Lilium wants the average person to be able to call for their air taxi with the push of a button, jump in when it arrives at a nearby landing pad, and jet off to their chosen destination. Talk about a cool future by 2025!

Taking a flight into space today? The scramjet-powered Waverider might make that possible in the future.

Increasing Safety

Governments, industry, and aeronautical researchers are betting that air travel will greatly expand in the coming years. With all the extra flights that will be crossing our skies, safety is an important issue. Safety at the airport and in the air are not the only places that researchers have been looking to make improvements. Scientists and engineers are working on many ways to improve aeronautics for the future.

Almost everyone has experienced days that they consider disappointing because of the weather. But what about weather situations that shut down flights and are dangerous and life threatening? Right now, research teams are working on a glider craft that could send real-time information to the National Weather Service. The glider will be formed from carbon fiber and will measure about 3 feet (.94 m) wide. After it passes future testing, this craft could improve weather forecasting for those in the air and on the ground. Lives and property could be saved because of improved, earlier reports of upcoming dangerous weather.

Birds as Models

Aeronautical engineers designing twenty-first-century aerospace vehicles are going back to the birds. Birds use muscles to flex their feathers and wings into different positions as they fly. They instinctively know how to hold their wings to get the best lift or to lower themselves when landing. Engineers and designers are trying to form aircraft wings that are just as movable and changeable. Using advanced technology, including computers, sensors, and special materials, researchers are hoping that their man-made wings will mimic this natural system.

Research teams depend on computers. A new system called ADATS is being tested to make data collection better. ADATS will speed up the amount of data that can be processed. When finished, this method would be like streaming eight high-definition movies in a second. Lots of data moving super fast would excite any scientist!

All in This Together

One way of looking at the future of aviation is to remember that it is a global issue. As a global community, we are all in this together—defining problems, testing new designs, and discovering the solutions. The Common Research Model (CRM) developed by NASA aims at giving aeronautical engineers and researchers a tool to provide help toward that global future.

Everyone working in the field of aviation can use this tool. The CRM exists as both an actual model plane and as a computer model. Many countries have already signed on to a special-use agreement. In some cases, the CRM has been sent to scientists for testing in their own wind tunnels. What could be a better idea than scientists and researchers from countries and governments around the globe working together on common issues of aviation?

One thing is certain: Scientists and engineers will continue experimenting in the field of aeronautics. As they define problems, ask questions, conduct experiments, collect data, and seek solutions, everyone's systems of aviation will soar into the future and become safer and more secure in the end.

CHRONOLOGY

1804

Sir George Cayley launches his model glider.

1866

Otto Lilienthal begins his aerodynamic testing.

1896

Samuel Langley flies the first unpiloted flying machine.

1903

The Wright brothers fly the first successful piloted airplane.

1976

The Concorde makes its first passenger flights.

1990

Boeing makes the 747-200, which currently serves as Air Force One.

2004

NASA's hypersonic scramjet flies at a record speed of Mach 10.

2009

First test flight of a jet with part biofuel-blend fuel.

2018

Target date to test the XB-1, or Baby Boom, supersonic jet.

2021

Target date to flight test the QueSST supersonic transport jet.

2025

Target date for Lilium's air taxi to be in service.

BIBLIOGRAPHY

Aerion Corporation. Retrieved September 10, 2017. www.aerionsupersonic.com/technology.

Airbus. Retrieved September 5, 2017. www.airbus.com.

Bilstein, Roger E. *Flight in America,* third ed. Baltimore, MD: Johns Hopkins University Press, 2001.

Boeing. Retrieved September 1, 2017. www.boeing.com.

Boom. Retrieved September 1, 2017. www.boomsupersonic.com.

Chow, Denise. "No Hands! Mind-Controlled Helicopter Flies on Brainwaves." Live Science, February 10, 2014. www.livescience.com/43250-mind-controlled-quadcopter.html.

Fingas, Jon. "Airbus Unveils an Autonomous, Modular Flying Car Concept." Engadget, March 8, 2017. www.engadget.com/2017/03/08/airbus-pop-up-flying-car-concept.

Kinney, Jeremy R. *Airplanes: The Life Story of a Technology.* Westport, CT: Greenwood Press, 2006.

LanzaTech. Retrieved September 1, 2017. www.lanzatech.com.

Mutzabaugh, Ben. "Boeing: 747's Future as a Passenger Aircraft Is Bleak." *USAToday,* June 20, 2017. www.usatoday.com/story/travel/flights/todayinthesky/2017/06/20/boeing-admits-its-747-queen-skies-has-no-future-passenger-plane/412666001.

NASA. Retrieved September 5, 2017. www.nasa.gov.

Overly, Steven. "The Concorde Failed to Change How We Fly, but It Still Could." *Washington Post,* February 13, 2017. www.washingtonpost.com/news/innovations/wp/2017/02/13/the-supersonic-flight-that-never-really-took-off-has-landed-for-good/?utm_term=.99d6eaed0cdf.

Bibliography

Raley, Dan. "Far Out." Boeing Frontiers, July 2016, pp. 18–23. www.boeing.com/news/frontiers/archive/2016/july/#/1.

Smithsonian National Air and Space Museum. "The Wright Brothers: The Invention of the Aerial Age." Retrieved September 2, 2017. www.airandspace.si.edu/exhibitions/wright-brothers/online.

Spenser, Jay. *The Airplane: How Ideas Gave Us Wings,* first ed. New York, NY: Smithsonian Books, 2008.

GLOSSARY

aerodynamics The study of how air flows around a plane.

aeronautics The study of the science of flight.

autonomous Having the ability of self control.

autopilot A setting or device that allows an airplane to fly automatically.

aviation The flying of airplanes.

biofuel Fuel made from sources other than oil, such as seeds, grain, or algae.

cambered Curved, as in a wing.

composite Made of different materials.

emission Substance given off into the air.

engineer A professional who designs and builds machines and structures.

glider A small airplane with no engine that uses air currents to keep flying.

Mach The ratio of the speed of an object to the speed of sound.

propulsion The force that moves something forward.

scramjet A propulsion system that gets its speed from oxygen in the atmosphere.

sonic boom An explosive noise caused when an aircraft travels faster than the speed of sound.

supersonic Faster than the speed of sound.

sustainable Using a resource in a way so that it is not depleted.

wing warping A system of twisting the edges of plane wings in opposite directions.

FURTHER READING

Books

Gaddi, Rosalie. *Austin's Airplane Adventure: Solve Problems Involving Measurement*. New York, NY: Powerkids Press, 2015.

Hayes, Amy. *How a Plane Is Made* (Engineering Our World). New York, NY: Gareth Stevens Publishing, 2016.

Hutchison, Patricia. *The Invention of the Airplane*. Mankato, MN: The Child's World, 2017.

Verstraete, Larry. *Innovations in Transportation*. New York, NY: Crabtree Publishing Company, 2017.

Websites

NASA Glenn Research Center: The Beginner's Guide to Aeronautics

www.grc.nasa.gov/www/k-12/airplane/index.html

Learn all about aeronautics.

Smithsonian National Air and Space Museum

www.howthingsfly.si.edu/forces-flight

Learn more about the four forces of flight.

INDEX